AUGUSTUS

Leaders of the Ancient World

AUGUSTUS

Margaux Baum and
Fiona Forsyth

ROSEN
PUBLISHING

New York

Published in 2017 by The Rosen Publishing Group, Inc.
29 East 21st Street, New York, NY 10010

First Edition

Library of Congress Cataloging-in-Publication Data

Names: Baum, Margaux, author. | Forsyth, Fiona, author.
Title: Augustus / Margaux Baum and Fiona Forsyth.
Description: First edition. | New York : Rosen Publishing, [2017] | Series: Leaders of the ancient world | Includes bibliographical references and index. | Audience: Grades 7–12.
Identifiers: LCCN 2016030405 | ISBN 9781508172420 (library bound)
Subjects: LCSH: Augustus, Emperor of Rome, 63 B.C.–14 A.D.—Juvenile literature. | Emperors—Rome—Biography—Juvenile literature. | Rome—History—Augustus, 30 B.C.–14 A.D.—Juvenile literature.
Classification: LCC DG279 .F67 2017 | DDC 937/.07092 [B] —dc23
LC record available at https://lccn.loc.gov/2016030405

Manufactured in Malaysia

CONTENTS

INTRODUCTION

O f the great civilizations of antiquity, few have had the same impact on the Western world as that of the Romans. Rome began as a minor city-state on the peninsula that would eventually become modern Italy. It had gone from being a monarchy, ruled by kings with absolute power, to a republic in which power was shared among a ruling class who owned property, a system that was influenced by but far more complex than the more direct form of Greek democracy.

Even as a republic, Rome grew in power and influence. From the Italian peninsula, aided by efficient government at home and its outposts all throughout the Mediterranean region and Europe, as well as a military that was well organized, well led, and powerful, it absorbed territory to become among the most powerful nations of its age.

The man we call Augustus became the first emperor of Rome and lived from 63 BCE to 14 CE. From the age of eighteen, when he became involved in politics, he lived a life carefully planned and orchestrated for its maximum effect on the Roman people.

The era of his rule and that of his descendants and successors, despite its origins in bloody

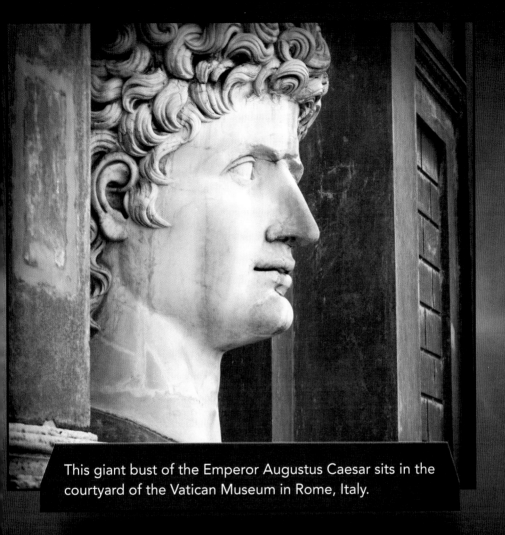

This giant bust of the Emperor Augustus Caesar sits in the courtyard of the Vatican Museum in Rome, Italy.

conflict, also ushered in an age of relative peace within the Empire itself called the Pax Romana ("the peace of Rome"). This inner peace, however, was also accompanied by very successful military expansion campaigns. Under Augustus, Rome ushered in an age when Rome would grow to its greatest extent. His reign added Egypt, much of the modern Balkan peninsula, and parts of Central Europe, along with an expansion into Germania and the full conquest of Hispania, the Roman name for the Iberian peninsula.

Augustus made a huge difference to the world of ancient Rome. He established a uniform currency system, a postal service, and a highway system along with bridges, aqueducts, and other structures that vastly increased the efficiency of the empire, and arguably improved the lives of all Roman subjects. For this, Augustus is remembered as an administrative genius whose efforts fostered communication and trade. He was also a patron of architecture and the arts. These aspects of his rule are celebrated, even as historians have noted his early years being marked by ruthlessness and cruelty, too.

The historians call his era the Age of Augustus, and during this age Rome raised great tributes in marble to its past and present leaders, raising them up to the status of gods on Earth. In fifty years, Augustus transformed himself and his city and the new empire.

HEIR TO POWER

Rome was a republic when Gaius Octavius—the future Gaius Julius Caesar Octavianus—was born in 63 BCE. This was a notable form of government for the ancient world, most of which was ruled by authoritarian leaders like monarchs, or kings. The word "republic" itself derives from *res publica*, which translates approximately as "public affairs" in Latin, the language of the Romans. For several centuries, a complicated system of representational government made sure that no one individual had too much power. This system had been set up because of the Romans' bad experiences earlier in their history, when they were ruled by kings who had abused their absolute power. The kings were deposed, or thrown out, with many Romans vowing never to be ruled by a monarch again.

LIKE FATHER, LIKE SON

When Gaius Octavius the younger (the future Augustus) was born, he inherited his father's name, and a cognomen, Thurinus. The cognomen was anickname that Roman nobles were given or adopted to commemorate some aspect of their personality, or a political or military triumph.

In the case of the Gaius Octavius Thurinus, it is likely that his father was memorializing a slave rebellion in Thurii, a city in southern Italy, around 60 BCE. The Roman Senate sent Gaius Octavius the elder to put down the rebellion. He was successful, and the victory bode well for his future political prospects. Military service, especially competent service which yielded victories, was one of the most surefire ways to move up in Roman politics. This was especially true during an era of great political turbulence. It was also very necessary, since the sheer size of the Empire around the time that the young Gaius Octavius was born demanded constant vigilance against rebellions.

Instead, every year men were chosen in elections to fill the offices that kept the state running on a day-to-day basis. If you were male, an adult, and a citizen of Rome, you had the right to vote in these elections.

The men who held office were automatically admitted to the Senate, a sort of council with about five hundred men in it. The Senate discussed public affairs and gave advice to the officers and the people of Rome about passing laws.

Because you had to be rich and wellborn to become a candidate for office, the Senate was more powerful than a council that just gave advice. Being wealthy and knowing all the other wealthy people gave you a clear advantage in practically any society.

The Senate did not have things its own way all the time, however. Special groups of ten men, called tribunes, were chosen by the people every year to keep an eye on the Senate and make sure that the interests of the ordinary people of Rome were protected. This system was beginning to break down when Augustus was born. Some individuals wanted more power for themselves and did not want to play by the rules. These individuals were able to maneuver and exploit the Roman political system by building power bases in its far-flung provinces. As Rome had grown from its foundation, traditionally dated at 753

BCE, it had conquered many lands, which were then called provinces.

At the time of Julius Caesar, these provinces stretched from modern Spain and France to Turkey and into North Africa. Roman officials would be sent to govern these provinces, and taxes would be raised and sent back to Rome. These provinces were controlled with a large army divided into legions. As legions were dispatched to areas of unrest, there was an opportunity for the commanders leading them to make themselves more powerful by building up a strong relationship with their troops. Once the soldiers owed more loyalty to an individual commander than to Rome, the commanders were in a position to make demands.

This naturally had a great effect on Augustus and his generation, for a change of this sort rarely comes about without violence. For the first eighteen years of his life, Augustus watched individuals build up their personal power and destroy the republican system. He saw politics turn violent. He saw civil war break out when he was thirteen years old, caused in part by his own great-uncle, Julius Caesar, who refused to give way to another general, Pompey. Fortunately for Augustus, Caesar won that particular struggle. When Augustus was eighteen, Julius Caesar was given the unheard-of title *dictator perpetuus*, meaning "dictator for life." This was a very dangerous step for Julius Caesar to take, for the office of dictator in the Roman Republic was conceived of only as an emergency measure. It was supposed to be held for a maximum of six months so that a crisis could be dealt with and the republic returned to normal.

By taking this title for life, Julius Caesar was undermining the republic and, some people said, aiming to make himself a king. This was the reason why men like Brutus and Cassius, who were colleagues and even personal friends of Caesar, felt that they had to assassinate him. They hoped that the republic would be restored, but they made a grave misjudgment. There were too many ambitious men who felt they could succeed where Caesar had failed.

THE GREAT NEPHEW

In 63 BCE, a young Roman politician called Gaius Octavius was doing very well for himself. He was climbing the ladder of offices that led to the top rung of Roman politics. This ladder was called the *cursus honorum*, and at the top was the office everyone hoped to get—consul. Gaius Octavius wasn't there yet, but he was likely to be a candidate for the office of praetor in a year or two, and after being praetor for a year you were rewarded with a governorship. As Rome had grown more powerful, it had conquered other lands around the Mediterr an ean and turned them into provinces of its empire. Officials got their first taste of provincial life when, after holding the praetorship, they governed a small province for a year before coming back to Rome and trying to be elected consul.

Competition was strong for all these offices, but Gaius Octavius was confident of success. He was from a respectable family, he had money, and his wife, Atia, was related to the Julius family, one of the oldest in Rome. Atia's uncle, Julius Caesar, was also beginning to make a name for himself in politics, and Gaius Octavius looked to him for help up the cursus honorum. Gaius Octavius had all the connections he needed to make his way in Roman politics. To crown it all, on September 23, 63 BCE, Atia gave birth to a son. Every Roman wanted a son to carry on the family name, so Gaius Octavius must have been very proud. The baby was named after his father, Gaius Octavius. He had two elder sisters, one of whom was a half sister from his father's previous marriage. The boy was especially close to his full sister, Octavia, and they remained close for the rest of their lives.

When young Gaius Octavius was four years old, his father died and his mother went on to marry Lucius Marcius Philippus, who became consul in 56 BCE. Julius Caesar also took an interest in his young great-nephew. He had no son of his own, and the young Octavius was very likely to be adopted as his heir. As Julius Caesar moved into the final phase of his own struggle for power, Octavius was given a taste of what was in store for him. In 46 BCE, at the age of sixteen, he went to Spain to join his great-uncle in one of the campaigns of the civil war. He so impressed Caesar that he decided to take the boy with him on his next campaign to Parthia, in Asia. Caesar had returned to Rome to make the arrangements for the campaign there, but he also had officers gathering and training troops at Apollonia, a town on the west coast of Greece. Gaius Octavius was sent there to observe the training of the soldiers and continue his education with the Greek teachers of Apollonia.

HEIR TO CAESAR

While he was in Apollonia, however, everything changed for Octavius. The news was brought from Rome that Julius Caesar had been killed by a group of conspirators led by his friend Marcus Brutus. Caesar's great-nephew was faced with a critical choice. Should he go back to claim his place as Caesar's heir, or should he wait in Greece to see what happened in Rome? If he returned to Rome without a clear idea of the situation, he might be walking

into a very dangerous and violent situation. But if he waited, others might seize the initiative and put him on the sidelines, too young and inexperienced to matter. Octavius decided to return.

At this point, few people in Rome knew much about Octavius or even cared. At the age of eighteen, Roman men still had a long way to go before they achieved a position of authority or power,

Vincenzo Camuccini painted *The Death of Julius Caesar*, this 1808 depiction of Caesar's assassination on the floor of the Roman Senate.

and they were expected to treat their elders with respect and wait their turn. Octavius knew he would have difficulty making people take him seriously, so he had to think of some unusual ways of attracting attention. He began with his name. He knew that Caesar had intended to adopt him and make him his heir. Caesar should have made all this clear in his will, but that was in the possession of Caesar's friend Mark Antony in Rome. Octavius decided to start calling himself Gaius Julius Caesar Octavianus. The "Octavianus" was to show that he had originally come from the Octavius family, and modern historians find it useful to call him Octavian because it helps to distinguish him from his great-uncle. But the young man himself preferred the name Caesar. This was his first change of name, and it shows that he already knew the power of names and titles. Julius Caesar's old soldiers would flock to support a boy with the name Caesar.

Octavian gathered support from these veteran soldiers as he crossed from Apollonia to southern Italy, and then traveled north to Rome. As he went, he learned more about his great-uncle's death and the tense situation in Rome. Marcus Brutus and Cassius, the leaders of the plot to kill Caesar, had been pardoned for the sake of keeping order. Caesar's friend Mark Antony was consul and was taking over in Rome. He controlled all of Caesar's papers, including his will, although copies of the will were available and confirmed what Caesar had intended regarding his great-nephew. Some

This bust of Augustus Caesar is one of many representations of the emperor scattered worldwide.

politicians, led by the elderly statesman Marcus Tullius Cicero, were trying to move away from the one-man rule instituted by Caesar and to restore the republic. Everyone was moving very cautiously. It was on this scene that Caesar's heir appeared.

Young Octavian began by approaching Mark Antony. The biographer Plutarch, who lived in the second century CE, describes their meeting in his *Life of Antony*:

> He immediately greeted Antony as a friend of his uncle and reminded him of the property in Antony's safe-keeping. For each Roman was owed 75 drachmas under the arrangements of Caesar's will. Antony at first, thinking little of him because of his youth, told him that he was not thinking straight.

Antony was not the only Roman to underestimate the young Caesar. In this rejection we see the beginnings of a conflict between the two men that had far-reaching effects.

Despite the lack of help from Antony, Octavian began to fulfill the terms of his adopted father's will. This involved dispersing a sum of money to every Roman citizen, so it gained him a great deal of popularity—especially when he let it be known that he was financing it himself because Antony was slow to release Caesar's funds. Octavian also held some athletic games to celebrate Julius Caesar, and something very unusual happened. The historian Suetonius, in his *Life of the God Julius*, tells us:

> A star shone for seven days continuously, rising at about the eleventh hour, and it was believed that it was Caesar's soul as he was received into heaven.

This star is now thought to have been a comet, but it had a profound effect on the Romans. It was certainly one of the reasons that Julius Caesar was later made a god. When the Senate officially deified Caesar in 42 BCE, Octavian was able to call himself by another title—*divi filius*, "son of a god." Divine ancestry became another justification for Octavian's struggle for power.

CLUTCHING AT POWER

Octavian wasted no more time on Antony for the

time being and formed a friendship with Marcus Tullius Cicero instead. Cicero had always been a supporter of the republican style of government. He did not see eye-to-eye with Antony and had supported Brutus and Cassius. The young Octavian found himself friends with a man who had approved of Caesar's murder! But Cicero proved very useful. He was a public speaker of considerable ability, and his series of speeches against Antony in the autumn of 44 BCE did a great deal to turn public opinion against Antony. Antony was forced to set off for his province in northern Italy toward the end of the year.

At the end of 44 BCE, Antony's consulship expired, and Octavian found out that Cicero was quite capable of going against the rules of the republic when it suited him. Cicero ensured that the young man was allowed unheard-of privileges. He was allowed to join the Roman Senate at a very young age, and he was given the powers of a praetor. Cicero kept up his barrage of hostility toward Antony in the Senate. Octavian eventually found himself assisting in an expedition to fight Mark Antony in northern Italy. He was nineteen years old. Like Antony, Cicero had

This illustration depicts Marcus Tullius Cicero condemning Lucius Catiline for a plot by the latter to murder the consuls and take over the government of Rome.

underestimated him. Cicero is reported to have said of Octavian:

Laudandum, ornandum, tollendum
(Praise him, flatter him, flatten him)

In this campaign, Octavian enjoyed two advantages. First, he had the name of Caesar, and second, his youth prevented people from realizing just how ruthless and ambitious he really was. When both consuls were killed during the campaign against Antony, Octavian took over the army, marched back to Rome, and demanded the consulship. The biographer Suetonius writes:

> When he was nineteen he took over the consulship by moving his troops threateningly close to the city of Rome, and by sending men to demand the consulship in the name of the army. And when the Senate hesitated, a centurion called Cornelius, the leader of the party, drew back his cloak and displayed the hilt of his sword, saying in the Senate-house without any hesitation, "This will do it if you don't."

Octavian himself tells a simpler, more flattering story. In his own *Res Gestae*, the account of his deeds written long after this time, Augustus the emperor says of himself as Octavian the young general:

> The people made me consul when
> both consuls had fallen in battle.

A NEW ALLIANCE

Octavian had heard of the less than flattering comments Cicero had made behind his back, and he decided that Cicero was not to be trusted anymore. Octavian felt no particular loyalty to Cicero or the Senate, and contacted Mark Antony. Together with another Roman politician, Lepidus, he and Antony met and decided to take control of Rome. They passed a law announcing themselves as a committee of three, a triumvirate, and said they were going to restore the republic.

The triumvirs set themselves up legally using the lawmaking process of Rome, but they decided among themselves which one would hold the consulship for the next five years. They also controlled all the troops in the empire. They began their rule by killing and exiling all who stood in their way. Among the victims of this purge were Antony's uncle and Lepidus's brother, both of whom escaped into exile, and Cicero, who at the age of sixty-three was murdered as he tried to flee. The official name for this purge was proscription. According to Cassius Dio, Antony ordered that Cicero's head and hands be cut off and displayed in the center of Rome as:

> A sight to make the Romans shiver,
> because they thought they saw not
> the image of Cicero's face so much as
> the image of Antony's soul.

ALLIES AND ENEMIES

Now just nineteen years old, Gaius Julius Caesar Octavianus was no longer an obscure figure. He had shown himself a legitimate heir to his famous uncle by ascending to consul of Rome at such a young age. With Antony and Lepidus as allies, he had begun the process of solidifying his power over Rome's government.

There was no time for Gaius Octavian to contemplate his achievements. He had to keep consolidating his relations with Rome and its army, and one of the best ways to do that was to show that he was still mindful of his adopted father. To the Romans, duty to one's parents was very important. That Gaius Octavian was not Caesar's natural son did not matter. He still had to show filial piety. In his *Res Gestae*, it is clear that avenging Caesar was now a priority.

> I drove into exile the men who
> slaughtered my father, gaining rep-
> aration for their crime by the due
> course of law. I later defeated them
> twice in battle as they waged war
> against the republic.

Octavian used the support of Lepidus and Antony to pursue Brutus and Cassius and defeat them at the Battle of Philippi in 42 BCE. Once he had avenged Julius Caesar, he made a solemn vow that he would build a temple in Rome dedicated to Mars the Avenger, the Roman god of war. You can still see the remains of this temple in the heart of modern Rome.

Octavian now found that it was no longer possible to restore the republic properly and retire from public life. He was still only twenty-one and a triumvir. He had youth and ambition, and he now turned his attention to the other members of the partnership.

It was clear that Lepidus provided nothing more than a buffer between the two real forces in the triumvirate, Antony and Octavian. He was an ineffectual person, always wavering before inevitably making the wrong choice. When he and Octa-

This statue of Augustus stands in Rome, Italy, on the Via dei Fori Imperiali.

vian were working to rid the seas of a pirate called Sextus Pompeius, Lepidus made an attempt to upstage Octavian and completely failed. He was forced out of office.

Octavian and Antony spent the ten years after the Battle of Philippi circling each other cautiously. Antony spent a good deal of time in the eastern end of the empire, while Octavian looked after the west and Italy. One crisis was weathered in 41 BCE when Antony's wife, Fulvia, and his brother Lucius Antonius led a rebellion in Italy while Antony was away. Octavian had to deal with this and did so effectively—some said even brutally. Lucius Antonius took refuge in the Italian town of Perusia, which Octavian besieged and captured. Suetonius tells us what happened:

> When Perusia was taken, he pun-
> ished many people, answering every
> one of them, as they tried to ask for
> pardon or to excuse themselves,
> with one reply, "You must die."

Antony himself was seriously embarrassed by his brother and wife, for he had not known what they intended. He and Octavian had to meet to

THE FINAL BATTLE, FOR NOW

The Battle of Phillipi was the final battle in what many historians would later call the Wars of the Second Triumvirate—that is, the conflict between the forces loyal to Mark Antony and Octavian (of the Second Triumvirate) and those loyal to Marcus Junius Brutus and Gaius Cassius Longinus. A big part of the motive from Octavian's perspective was, certainly, to avenge Julius Caesar's assassination. For the Romans of this era, this was as pivotal a conflict as Pearl Harbor would be for Americans in World War II.

In October of 42 BCE, two large Roman armies were massing in the plains west of Phillipi, an ancient city in the region of the empire known as Macedonia. Octavian's enemies had certain advantages, and in the early part of the battle, which took place over a few week's time, it seemed they had the advantage. Brutus even diverted a river to flood the camps of his enemies. Apparently, even Octavian had to be evacuated before one skirmish, because he had fallen very ill during the conflict. However, in the end, they were beaten back. In defeat, Brutus and Cassius both committed suicide. Mark Antony and Octavian split the empire among them and began an uneasy peace.

Johann Heinrich Tischbein the Elder created this painting of Egyptian queen Cleopatra embracing Mark Antony.

patch things up. Antony married Octavian's sister Octavia as a sign of good faith. As the years passed, however, it became apparent that a crisis was approaching. Antony and Octavian could not exist as equal rulers of Rome for much longer.

The crisis came to a head when Antony embarked on an affair with Cleopatra, the queen of Egypt, and sent home Octavia. Octavian considered it an insult. Antony was rarely in Italy, and Octavian played on this by spreading rumors that Antony was living an extravagant life in Egypt. The Romans, priding themselves on their hardworking and austere lifestyles, did not react favorably to the idea that one of their greatest generals was growing soft in the East. Octavian's masterstroke was to find and read out the will that Antony had left in Rome. In it, Antony made his children by Cleopatra his heirs. He had abandoned his Roman wife and Roman children.

Octavian now prepared for war. During the previous decade, his troops had successfully faced threats from the people of the Balkan area of Europe and from the navy of Sextus Pompeius. Octavian and his supporters were now experienced in warfare. Octavian's friend Marcus Agrippa had shown real skill as a general, and under his supervision a huge naval base was constructed in the Bay of Naples.

Ships were prepared and men trained, and in 31 BCE, Antony and Octavian met in a sea battle near the western coast of Greece, at a place called Actium. A poet of the Augustan Age, Virgil, gives us a glamorous description of Octavian in *The Aeneid*:

> Here was Caesar Augustus, leading Italy into battle, standing on the prow of his ship, accompanied by the Senate and people, the gods of the family and the great gods, a double light streaming from his face and his father's star shining over him.

Octavian won the Battle of Actium. Antony and Cleopatra

This mural conveys the epic scale of combat of the Battle of Actium in September of 31 BCE. The decisive victory by Octavian allowed him to consolidate his imperial power.

fled to Egypt, abandoning their fleet. The historian Velleius Paterculus sums up the shame Romans must have felt when he says:

> Cleopatra takes the first prize for running away. Antony preferred the company of the fleeing queen to that of the fighting soldier.

In Rome, Marcus Tullius Cicero, the son of the man Antony had killed thirteen years earlier, became consul. All statues of Mark Antony were removed. The Battle of Actium did not produce total victory for Octavian. He first had to deal with mutiny among his troops, and then he had to pursue Antony and Cleopatra back to Alexandria, Cleopatra's headquarters in Egypt. In the end, both Antony and Cleopatra committed suicide when Alexandria fell, and Octavian was free to take over Egypt. He had Cleopatra's son by Julius Caesar, Caesarion, put to death. Octavian had no intention of sharing his precious legacy as Caesar's son with anyone else. Antyllus, son of Antony and Antony's first wife, Fulvia, was also put to death. But Antony's other children—Iullus Antonius, son of Antony and Fulvia; and Cleopatra, Alexander,

Cleopatra and her son Caesarion are depicted in this engraving, in which the she presents her child to the Egyptian gods. Octavian ordered him killed at age seventeen.

and Ptolemy, children of Antony and Cleopatra—were not judged to be a threat because they were too young. They needed a home and, surprisingly, the woman Antony had rejected, his wife Octavia, took them in to add to her own four children. That Octavia managed this large brood when there was so much potential for hurt and embarrassment says a lot about her.

This seventeenth-century painting by Sébastien Bourdon, *Augustus Before the Tomb of Alexander the Great*, shows the visit of the conquering Augustus to this symbolic site.

By conquering Egypt, Octavian had transformed the economy of the Roman world. Egypt was very rich, and Octavian himself became very wealthy. Egypt also supplied Rome with a great deal of wheat, and Octavian decided to take Egypt officially into the Roman Empire to ensure the supply of this wheat. So much money entered into the Roman economy after the invasion of Egypt that interest rates on loans went down to a third of what they had been!

Eventually, in 29 BCE, Octavian returned to Rome and celebrated. Once more he had to be careful about Antony, for it would have been very tasteless to celebrate a victory against a fellow Roman. On three successive days, Octavian held processions, known as triumphs, to celebrate three victories: his campaign in central Europe and the conquests at Actium and Alexandria. A triumph was a military honor awarded to a successful general by decree of the Senate. The general and his soldiers would march through Rome, cheered by the people, and make sacrifices to the god Jupiter in thanksgiving for their victory.

Velleius Paterculus gives a very enthusiastic summary of the state of the *res publica*, the republic, under Octavian:

> There is nothing man can ask from the gods, nothing the gods can offer man, nothing a heart can desire or good fortune bring to pass, that after his return to the city Augustus did not accomplish for the res publica, the Roman people, and the world.

THE DAWN OF EMPIRE

Even a leader as single-minded and ambitious as Octavian may have fallen short of his goals if not for the support of those close to him. There were three in particular who had helped him face the crises and chaos as he took power and ushered in the new imperial era of Rome. Among the most important was his general (and friend), Marcus Vipsanius Agrippa. While he was a skilled soldier and statesman, as well as being an architect, he was also pragmatic and loyal, and was content to be Octavian's second-in-command without resentment.

Another valuable ally, and one more attuned to the internal intrigues of power in Rome itself, was Gaius Maecenas. Maecenas analyzed the divisions and alliances among Roman politicians and leaders, as well as public opinion,

This marble bust shows the Roman statesman and general Marcus Vipsanius Agrippa.

and advised Octavian on how to react. He also had considerable diplomatic and administrative skills, and was particularly known as the one who influenced greatly the emperor's patronage for the arts.

Livia was a remarkable woman, particularly in a society in which women had little official power and few rights. Her marriage to Octavian had caused a minor scandal in 42 BCE. The historian Tacitus tells us:

> Caesar, inflamed with passion for her, took her away from her husband. It is not known whether or not she was unwilling, and he was so eager that he took her into his home while she was still pregnant, without even waiting for her to give birth.

Octavian had already divorced his first wife, Scribonia, just as she gave birth to their daughter, saying that he was tired of being nagged. But Suetonius says of Octavian's feelings for Livia:

> He loved her and respected her above all others to the end of his life.

As for Livia, she gave some useful advice when asked later how she influenced her husband:

> She answered that she was completely
> faithful, did whatever pleased him
> with good humor, never interfered
> in his business, and pretended to
> neither hear of nor find out about his
> "bits on the side."

This painted wall is inside the Roman villa that once belonged to the spouse of Augustus, Livia Drusilla, also known as Julia Augusta.

Octavian and Livia had no children of their own, but Octavian's daughter from his former marriage, Julia, had several children. Octavian, as we shall see, valued these grandchildren highly and even adopted some of them to give himself heirs.

NEW BEGINNINGS

Now the four of them—Agrippa, Maecenas, Livia, and Octavian—planned the consolidation of Octavian's power. The turbulent past had to be buried, and people had to be persuaded to look forward. The celebratory triumphs helped to cheer the people, and other commemorations took place. Octavian founded a city at Actium and called it Nicopolis (victory city), while in Rome an arch was built in the Forum Romanum, a civic center with temples, shops, a Senate house, and speakers' platforms. The Romans used huge arches as memorials to great events, placing them in prominent positions and decorating them with carvings and statues.

Along with the celebrations came reminders of the blessings of peace, and the Senate took an important step here. Augustus himself in the *Res Gestae* says proudly:

Our ancestors had decided that
when peace had been achieved on
land and sea throughout the whole
empire of the Roman people the
Temple of Janus should be closed.
In all the time from the foundation
of Rome to my birth, according to
tradition, this had happened twice.
The Senate decreed it should be shut
three times during my time as leading citizen.

Octavian also finished a building project
started by Julius Caesar, a new Senate house in the
Forum. There were games, gladiator fights, and ani-
mal hunts as part of the celebrations. The historian
Cassius Dio says that this was the first time that
Rome had seen a rhinoceros or hippopotamus.

In 29 BCE, Octavian took on a very difficult
task—that of checking the credentials of the men
in the Senate. Traditionally this job fell to an official
called a censor. It was necessary to make sure that
the Senate was composed of men of the right sort
of birth and wealth, and that senators behaved in
a way that was fitting for their rank. A censor also
had the power to make sure that the Senate was

The remains of the Roman Forum are shown here. There and elsewhere, Augustus erected structures honoring his reign.

filled with men who would be supporters of that censor in the future. This would be very important if that censor wanted to enact some extraordinary measures, as Octavian planned to do. According to Dio, fifty senators quietly withdrew from the Senate and a hundred and forty others retired under compulsion. Octavian also introduced the rule that senators could not travel outside Italy without permission. Now Octavian could always be sure where potential opponents were.

In 28 BC, Octavian enacted a law that invalidated everything he had done while a triumvir! Suetonius says:

> Since in the period of civil strife and
> wars he had enacted many deeds
> that went beyond the law and jus-
> tice, especially when he had ruled
> jointly with Antony and Lepidus, he
> abolished all these in one law.

This seemed like a very dangerous admission from Octavian. Was he inviting people to criticize him for acts of the triumvirate such as the proscriptions? Making this law was probably Octavian's way of showing the Roman people that the bad old days were gone and could be forgotten. Certainly, with the abolition of the triumvirate's deeds, Octavian was ready to move onto his most important reform.

NEGOTIATING AUTHORITY

Octavian's official power had rested in two positions: the consulship, which he held continuously from 31 to 23 BCE, and the triumvirate, now abolished. But he had many other sources of power, which, while not legal, were very persuasive. Being Caesar's heir had helped him, as had Caesar's deification. After the capture of Alexandria, of course, Octavian also had the wealth of Egypt and he controlled the troops. All this combined to give him a large amount of what the Romans called *auctoritas*, the power commanded through the respect other people have for you and your achievements and abilities. In 27 BCE, both official power and auctoritas were put to the test when Octavian took what seemed like a huge risk. He walked into the Senate and announced his resignation.

How could the Senate have responded to this bombshell? They could have taken the opportunity to reestablish the republic, of course, but it was

MIXED FEELINGS

The following two passages illustrate the different views Romans took of Augustus. The first is Augustus's own account in the *Res Gestae*. The second is that of the historian Tacitus, writing at the start of the second century AD. Augustus writes:

> In my sixth and seventh consulships [28 and 27 BCE], after I had put an end to civil war and taken control of the state with the agreement of all, I transferred the rule of the res publica from my own control to the authority of the Senate and the people of Rome. To reward me for this, the Senate decreed that I should be called by the name Augustus, that the doorposts of my house should be publicly decorated with laurel, and the civic crown hung over my door, and that the golden shield be placed in the Julian Senate House, which declares in its inscription that it was given to me by the Senate and people of Rome on account of my courage, mercy, justice, and sense of duty. After this time, I outshone everyone in auctoritas, but had no more power than the other men who were my colleagues in office.

Tacitus writes:

When he had won over the army with
money and the people with grain, and
everyone with the sweet feeling of peace,
little by little he began to move, taking
upon himself the duties of the Senate, the
offices of state and the law. No one opposed
him: Men of real spirit had died either
in battle or the proscriptions, while the
rest of the upper classes according to how
eagerly they queued up for servitude were
rewarded with gifts and honors. Once they
benefited from the new state of affairs, they
preferred to be safe in the present than risk
the dangers of the past.

almost impossible for this to happen now, and the
Senate knew it as well as Octavian did. Despite his
resignation, he did not intend to give up any real
power. He and his friends had worked out a way of
ensuring that he remained in control, and for some
of the senators Octavian's announcement was not a
surprise. As the cries of protest rang out, Octavian
allowed himself to be convinced to stay on, and as

he did so, he quietly made more changes.

Octavian continued to serve as consul, to make sure that he was always at the helm of the state. He reorganized the government of some provinces. Egypt, for example, was very important, and Octavian did not want to let a senator govern it. The solution was to let it be governed by a person who did not normally hold such power and who would be very grateful to Octavian. So he decreed that Egypt was to be governed by a member of the *equites*, the class below the senatorial class. Equites were the business class of Rome, the men who ran trade and took contracts from the state to collect taxes. They did not normally enjoy the prestige enjoyed by senators, but governing Egypt would give one member of that class a taste of that prestige. Octavian himself supervised other provinces that were unstable enough to need the presence of the army and appointed hand-picked senators. Finally, Octavian graciously accepted a new name carefully proposed by a senator, and became Augustus. The name was not his first choice, according to Dio:

> Caesar was very keen to be called
> Romulus, but when he realized that
> this made people suspicious that he

actually wanted to become king, he no longer went after this, but was called Augustus, a name indicating that he was more than human, for everything revered and holy is called august.

Romulus was the founder and first king of Rome, and Augustus wanted to share in the idea of founding the city. Unfortunately, the idea of a

This marble statue on a pedestal in Siena, Italy, shows the mythical founders of Rome, Romulus and Remus, who were said to have been raised by a wolf.

king was still strongly opposed by the people of Rome, and Julius Caesar's assassination could not be ignored. So Augustus he became, and Augustus Caesar was how he was known for the rest of his life. This transformation was accepted with mixed feelings.

Other changes were made as Augustus and his friends gradually acquired more power and as circumstances forced change. In 23 BC, for example, Augustus resigned the consulship and did not feel the need to hold it continuously again. He had realized that by holding one of the two consulships every year, he was blocking one way in which senators could gain glory and fulfill ambition for themselves. A plot against him, formed by some dissatisfied senators, probably encouraged him to think of this way of appeasing the Senate. Instead of the consulship, Augustus took the office that appealed to the people—an honorary tribune. He was not one of the ten official tribunes, but he enjoyed all the powers of a tribune for the rest of his life. These powers included the right to propose a law without having to consult the Senate. Augustus also assumed authority over all provincial governors so that he could intervene anywhere in the empire, not just in those provinces that he personally supervised.

Augustus was seriously affected by an unknown illness in 23 BCE. Dio describes a touching sickbed scene in which Augustus gathered the leading men of Rome around him and gave his ring to Agrippa. This was very significant. A Roman nobleman's ring held his seal, a carved gem that when imprinted in wax left an impression on important documents. It served as a signature does in legal documents today. When Augustus gave his ring to Agrippa, he put him in charge of official documents. Augustus recovered from this illness, but it raised a troublesome question for everyone: What would happen to Rome now if Augustus died?

BUILDING A NEW ROME

D uring the time of the Roman Republic, the most respected and senior member of the Senate had been known as the *princeps*, which translates roughly from Latin as "leading citizen." To keep up the appearance of republican government even as he had consolidated his imperial power over the state, Augustus took this as an unofficial title. Meanwhile, he allowed the Senate to meet, debate, and make recommendations on policy. Elections were still held every summer, and laws debated and passed. The courts decided cases, and by all accounts, things did not seem initially different than they had been.

Technically, Augustus's power was rooted in the old political structures of the republic. However, no one mentioned his absolute authority but nor did they seriously challenged it. The former republic was now an empire, but Augustus and his supporters pushed the notion that everything was the same.

Augustus advanced the idea that Rome was following the old traditions, and this is made clear in the laws he passed, the building schemes that were undertaken, and the literature that was produced during his rule. In these schemes, Augustus also managed to do a lot of good for ordinary Roman people, although he was not successful in everything he tried. One of his greatest failures was the campaign against the Germanic tribes of northern Europe. The Germanic tribes put up a stiff resistance to Roman expansion. In 9 CE, a general called Varus foolishly ventured too far into hostile territory and three entire legions were massacred—a disaster for Rome and Augustus, although both recovered.

Augustus himself was not so popular that no one disagreed with him, and he found, as many leaders do, that there were a few people willing to make attempts on his life. None of these men succeeded, and it is difficult to tell how serious a threat they really were. Also, Augustus's personal life was occasionally very unhappy. But none of

Arminius, a leader of the Cherusci, a Germanic tribe who often fought Rome, is shown here after beating the Roman Varus at the Battle of the Tuetoburg Forest, in 9 CE.

this detracts from his achievements. Augustus made changes in practically every aspect of Roman life, from passing a law to encourage an increase in the birthrate to having a channel of the river Tiber cleared of rubbish and widened to avoid flooding. He promoted his popularity with the citizens of Rome by handing out money, staging games, and constructing and refurbishing buildings. In the *Res Gestae*, he writes:

> According to the terms of my father's will, I gave out three hundred sestertii to each man of the Roman people. In 29 BCE, in my own name, I gave four hundred sestertii from the spoils of war. Again, in 24 BCE, I gave out four hundred sestertii to each man, and in 23 BCE I made twelve donations of grain bought at my own expense. In 12 BCE for the third time I gave four hundred sestertii.

To give you an idea of what kind of wealth this represented, an ordinary soldier in Augustus's time was paid 900 *sestertii* a year. To buy enough corn to feed that soldier for a year would cost about

240 sestertii. Augustus's handouts were sufficiently generous so that an ordinary family could buy enough basic food for several months.

Augustus also initiated a new building boom. As he says in the *Res Gestae*:

> I built the Senate-House and the Chalcidicum next to it, and the Temple of Apollo on the Palatine, along with its colonnades, the temple of the God Julius . . . I completed the Forum of Julius and the basilica which lies between the Temple of Castor and the Temple of Saturn, works which had been begun and abandoned by my father . . . In 28 BCE, at the decree of the Senate, I repaired eighty two temples in the city, and left out none that needed repair at the time . . .
> On land which I bought at my own expense, I built the Temple of Mars Ultor and the Forum of Augustus, using the spoils of war.

These building projects occupied prime land in the center of Rome and sometimes

This color engraving shows the Temple of Mars Ultor, which was constructed in the Forum of Augustus, as one of many new construction projects Augustus initiated.

involved years of building. The Temple of Mars Ultor, which Augustus vowed to build at the Battle of Philippi in 42 BCE, was not completed until 2 BCE.

Suetonius tells us that Augustus never hid his enjoyment of the games and gladiatorial shows. In this he was like most Romans. In the *Res Gestae*, Augustus writes:

> I put on gladiatorial games, three
> times in my own name and five times
> in the names of my sons or grand-
> sons. About ten thousand men fought
> in these games . . . I put on hunts of
> African wild animals twenty-six times,
> in circus or forum or amphitheater,
> either in my own name or the names
> of my sons or grandsons.

We do not have to rely on Augustus's own words to be convinced of the material benefits Rome enjoyed under his rule. Many of the stories Suetonius tells us about Augustus illustrate the range of measures in which he was personally involved.

He invented a system of guard-
ing against fires carried out by
night-watchmen . . . He took upon
himself to repair the Flaminian Way
as far as Ariminum, and divided up
the other road repairs to be done by
men who had celebrated triumphs, to
be paid for out of the wealth they had
gained in war . . . When there were
complaints about the short supply
and high price of wine, he said very
sternly, that his son-in-law Agrippa
had made sure that men would not
go thirsty by providing several aqueducts . . . He made his Forum rather
narrow, because he did not go as far
as to force the owners of the nearest
houses to leave.

And, sure enough, if you go to Rome today,
you will be able to walk around Augustus's Forum
and see the ingenious way in which its architect hid
the irregularities in the plan of the building—irregularities forced upon Augustus by the recalcitrant,
or resistant, homeowners nearby. What Suetonius
does not say, but what you will be able to see for

yourself, is the very high wall that Augustus had built between his Forum and those houses, as a firebreak perhaps, or to keep out of sight those who had thwarted the princeps.

Certainly the Forum bordered the Subura, one of the slums of Rome, where fires were frequent. But Augustus was very good at using his buildings to make statements. This very Forum contained a temple to Mars, the god of war (here called Mars Ultor, or Mars the Avenger), to remind people that Augustus had avenged the murder of his adopted father, Julius Caesar, at the Battle of Philippi. The Forum also held countless statues of Rome's heroes from bygone days and, of course, a statue of Augustus himself in front of the temple in the center. Augustus might have made a pretense of being just an ordinary man, but he expected no one to take him seriously about this.

ROME REIMAGINED

One of Augustus's most famous sayings, recorded by Suetonius, was that he found Rome a city of brick and left her a city of marble. This is an exaggeration, of course, but Augustus was right to be proud of his achievements. The work was not just decorative. The construction of aqueducts and a new set of public baths built by Agrippa must have had an impact on people's health. But there is no doubt that Augustus and Agrippa were determined to leave a permanent mark of stone on Rome. One such monument is worth discussing in further detail, to show how Augustus could make use of such buildings to promote himself.

The Ara Pacis Augustae is a very grand name meaning the "Altar of Augustan Peace." We hear of it in the *Res Gestae*:

> When after a successful expedition to
> Gaul and Spain I returned to Rome
> in 13 BCE, the Senate decreed that
> an altar of Augustan Peace should be
> consecrated on the Campus Martius,
> to give thanks for my return.

The altar was finally finished in 9 BCE. It stood outside the old city walls, in the area north of the city called the Campus Martius (Field of Mars), close to the main road into the city center, the Flaminian Way. It still stands on a bank of the Tiber River, moved a little way from its original position

The Ara Pacis Augustae (the "Altar of Augustan Peace")
was built between 13 BCE and 9 BCE and is now a
museum piece.

and partially restored by Italian archaeologists. The altar is guarded on all sides by a wall, which is full of carvings and sculptures on both sides, with the most impressive scenes on the outside.

One outside wall shows an elegant and elaborate carving of the spindly stems and leaves of an acanthus plant curled into beautiful patterns. Among the leaves, small animals and insects hide at just the right height for children to make a game of spotting them, and carved swans clap their wings overhead. Above this is carved a procession of people—priests and senators and members of Augustus's family—on their way to an important ritual, probably the sacrifice that dedicated the building of the altar itself in 13 BCE. Some of the people are solemn; some are chatting with each other. A young woman and her husband are being "shushed" by the old lady next to them. Children walk with their parents, one little boy anxiously hanging onto the cloak of the man in front of him so that he doesn't get lost. Augustus himself is walking with the priests while Agrippa, who, in 13 BCE, married Augustus's daughter, Julia, leads the family of the princeps. Augustus and Agrippa are easy to spot because they look like their portraits on coins, while the lady behind Agrippa is surely either Livia or Julia. Some of the faces are extremely realistic. One elderly senator in particular looks straight out at the viewer with a rather fed-up look on his face, as if he is tired of the ceremony already.

On either side of the entrances to the altar are carved panels. In one panel, the legendary hero Aeneas

This panel from the Ara Pacis Augustae displays the sacrifice of the mythological hero Aeneas to Di Penates, Roman deities that look after the household.

A POET IN THE SERVICE OF THE STATE

While architects improved the look of the city, cultural life was also flourishing. Augustus's friend Maecenas had been gathering a collection of gifted writers who were encouraged to use their talents in certain directions, which they were happy to do. The outstanding writer of this group was the poet Virgil, still regarded as one of the all-time greats of Western literature. Virgil's writings unashamedly celebrate the theme of Augustan peace and glorify Augustus himself. Today we might find it discomforting for a poet to glorify a politician, but we must remember that to many Romans the Age of Augustus was a welcome relief from the grinding years of war and poverty.

In one of his earliest poems, from a collection called *Eclogues*, we find out that Virgil had a special reason to be grateful to Augustus. In this poem, a young shepherd tells his friend that the family farm, which was confiscated from him, was returned to him by a young man. This had happened to Virgil's own family in the past. Augustus was still Octavian then, and the triumvirs were doing a fair amount of military campaigning. This meant that they needed a great deal of land on which to settle retired soldiers. The confiscation of land took place all over Italy, and many people were simply thrown

This Roman mosaic found in Hadrumetum, Tunisia, shows the poet Virgil (*center*) flanked by the muses of history and tragedy.

off their farms to make way for the soldiers. Virgil was lucky. Augustus's friend Maecenas returned his family's farm, and so the poet recorded his gratitude.

Virgil's greatest poem is *The Aeneid*, a long poem telling the story of the Trojan prince Aeneas. Centuries earlier, the Greek poet Homer had told the story of the Trojan War in his poem called *The Iliad*, and this would have been well known to every Roman schoolchild. Virgil wrote *The Aeneid* as a kind of sequel to *The Iliad*, and

(SIDEBAR CONTINUED ON THE NEXT PAGE)

it told the story of Aeneas's escape from Troy and his wandering around the Mediterranean before landing on the shores of Italy. There is no doubt that Virgil intended his readers to make comparisons between the hero of his epic and Augustus. In several prophetic passages, Aeneas is given a glimpse into the future of the nation he will found. In one such passage, Virgil glorifies the Roman Empire and the Augustan Age:

> Other peoples will more delicately coax
> living shape out of bronze, will draw out
> real faces from marble; they will plead cases
> better, will trace out the course of the heav-
> ens and foretell the rising of the stars. You
> Roman, make it your place to rule over the
> peoples with your empire and—these are
> your particular skills—to place tradition
> upon peace, to spare the conquered, and
> crush the arrogant with war.

makes a sacrifice upon reaching Italy. Aeneas supposedly escaped the destruction of Troy by the Greeks and came to Italy, where his descendant Romulus founded Rome. Romulus is also carved on the wall. Augustus was trying to convey the idea that he, too, was a founder of a new Rome. On another panel, a beautiful woman representing either the earth or the land of Italy sits amidst the fruit and the animals produced by the land, with two babies in her lap. The message here is clear—prosperity is returning to Italy under Augustus.

Here, many visitors to Rome would have had their first sight of Augustus, and it would have reminded them of the things that Augustus held dear—respect for religion, family values, and Rome's great past. There is one more trick to the altar. Nearby, on the Campus Martius, Augustus had set up a huge sundial, the pointer of which was an Egyptian obelisk. The shadow of this obelisk moved across a diagram etched on paving stones on the ground to tell the date and time of day. On Augustus's birthday, the tip of the shadow lay in the doorway of the Ara Pacis as a tribute to the builder. But beautiful though it was, the greatest symbolism lay in its name— the Altar of Augustan Peace.

Peace was not just something to be enjoyed by the Romans under Augustus. It was their duty to bring it to the world, by conquest if necessary. Augustus had brought a sense of destiny to his people.

FATHER OF THE EMPIRE

In 2 BCE, Augustus was sixty years old. The aging emperor received a special honor from the Senate: the title of *pater patriae*, Latin for "father of the country." The historian and biographer Suetonius reported that Augustus accepted the award at the ceremony literally weeping. He said:

> Fathers of the Senate, as I have
> achieved my dearest hope, what else
> have I to ask of the immortal gods
> except that it is allowed that I keep
> this universal backing of yours to
> the very end of my life.

At his advanced age, it seemed that everything had come full circle for Rome's first emperor. The Pax Romana was in full swing, with Rome enjoying a long stretch of stability and prosperity. The empire would not even reach its full extent until about a century later, under the emperor Trajan. In Rome itself, the temple of Mars in the Forum of Augustus was dedicated, another symbol of his power made solid and permanent.

In his private life, however, all was not well. Personal crises involving his family—especially his daughter, Julia—threatened to spill over into the political sphere.

During Augustus's reign, a Roman imperial mint was founded in Lugdunum, an ancient Roman city in Gaul (now Lyon, France). It produced this coin, depicting Augustus.

75

A QUESTION OF SUCCESSION

Normally, a Roman would look to his eldest son to be his heir and take over family and fortune. Julia was Augustus's only child, and in the absence of a crucial male heir she became important, especially as Augustus had so much more than most other Romans to leave to his heir. Not only did Augustus love her as his daughter, he knew that her future husband would be a very important man in the republic. The question of who would take over when Augustus died was not discussed in public, because it had not been established that Augustus's position as princeps would be a hereditary office. Rome was not a possession to be handed down from father to son, at least not officially.

And yet what else could happen? No other way of choosing a new leader had been set up, and the alternative, that Rome could somehow return to a republican government, was by now unworkable. So although everyone knew that Augustus would have to set up an heir who would take up the reins of power after his death, no one could actually say any-thing about it in public. It seems like a very strange, if not ridiculous, situation. Of course, behind the scenes, Augustus had been working to solve this problem for a long time. This is where the question of Julia came in, and in 23 BCE, she was married to Augustus's nephew Marcellus, the son of his sister Octavia. Unfortunately, the young man died very soon afterward. In 21 BCE, Julia was married to the faithful Marcus Agrippa. Even though he was not really the leader to follow Augustus, he was a safe choice until some other solution presented itself.

Agrippa provided the solution himself. He and Julia had a family of five, three sons and two daughters, before Agrippa died in 12 BCE. Augustus adopted two of these grandchildren, the eldest sons Gaius and Lucius, and it quickly became clear that these two boys were being groomed to take over from Augustus. He took personal care of their education and was clearly very proud of them. When they went through the coming-of-age ceremony that Roman boys went through at about fifteen, Augustus made sure that he was holding the consulship. Suetonius says that Augustus wanted to make sure that he was in this position when he introduced the boys to public life.

When Agrippa died, Julia was widowed for the second time. This time the lucky man to marry Julia was Tiberius, Livia's eldest son by her first marriage. Tiberius had been very young when his mother had left his father and married Augustus, and he had been brought up with his younger brother, Drusus, in the extended family created by the several marriages of Augustus, Livia, and Octavia. This meant that Tiberius would have known Julia, Marcellus, the two Antonias, the sons and daughters of Mark Antony, and even Cleopatra's children. This was the "imperial family."

Augustus used the younger members of this family in whatever way seemed useful to him and the republic. A tie formed by marriage was taken very seriously in Roman politics, and the more young men and women of the great families Augustus could get bound up with his own family, the better it was for him. Within the close circle of friends and relations around the princeps himself, marriages were a reward. For example, Tiberius was earlier married to Vipsania, Agrippa's daughter, and Drusus married the younger Antonia. Tiberius and Drusus proved invaluable additions to the imperial family, for they turned out to be very capable generals. It was good to be able to keep command of the troops in the family. Dru-

This bust shows Augustus's daughter, Julia the Elder.

sus unfortunately died from a wound in 9 BCE, but not before he had married Antonia and had three children, one of whom would become the fourth emperor, Claudius. Tiberius was unwilling to divorce Vipsania in order to marry Julia, but he did so anyway. No doubt his mother, the formidable Livia, persuaded him. Unfortunately, this did not help him build a happy relationship with Julia. Suetonius says:

> He was forced to divorce Agrippa's daughter and to marry Julia, the daughter of Augustus, without delay, which caused him great distress . . . After the divorce, he regretted that he had left her, and when it happened that he saw her once, he gazed after her with so much longing and tears in his eyes that care was taken to make sure that she did not come into his sight again.

At some point, Julia seems to have lost control of herself. She began a number of notorious love affairs and was seen at wild parties. On several occasions, she flaunted herself rather shock-

TIBERIUS CÆSAR.

TIberius Caesar was Roman emperor from 14 CE to 37 CE and was a stepson of Augustus. He is shown here wearing a laurel wreath, near the beginning of his reign.

ingly on the speakers' platform in the Roman Forum. In 6 BCE, Tiberius quietly retired from public life. We are not entirely sure why he did this, although Julia's behavior must have been very embarrassing, and perhaps he just wanted to be out of the way when Augustus found out. Perhaps he went off to sulk, annoyed at the obvious favor being shown to little Gaius and Lucius by Augustus. Whatever the reason, it left Augustus without the senior general of the Roman army, and there were not many men left in the family who had the maturity and experience to fill that role. Augustus wanted important work entrusted to those who were close to him, and Gaius and Lucius were just too young.

Tiberius's self-imposed exile must have annoyed Augustus greatly, especially as it came after he had granted Tiberius the powers of a tribune. It was a mark of high esteem. Only Marcus Agrippa had been similarly honored by Augustus. Suetonius describes the reaction of Tiberius:

> He used the excuse that he was worn
> out by the demands of his duties and
> needed rest, and so asked for some
> leave of absence; and he did not give

in either to his mother's pleading or to his stepfather's complaining that he was being abandoned—a complaint which Augustus even made in the Senate.

The arguments behind the scenes within the imperial family are not hard to imagine! After Tiberius had left, Julia's behavior became known to Augustus. The historian Velleius Paterculus could hardly believe the depths of her depravity. Augustus seems to have been very slow to believe what the rest of Rome had known for years, but finally he acted:

> His daughter Julia ignored what was due to her father and husband, and tried every form of wild or disgraceful behavior that can bring shame to the woman who does it or allows it. She judged the size of her fortune by the freedom it gave her to sin, claiming that whatever she wanted was right…Julia was banished to an island and removed from her father's sight.

THE HEIR APPARENT

By the end of 2 BCE, Augustus had no Agrippa or Maecenas, no Drusus or Tiberius, and no Julia. He still had Livia to advise him, but she was in favor of her own son, Tiberius. Only Gaius and Lucius were left to take up the reins of power after him.

From a very early age, Gaius and Lucius were brought into public life. Each boy had been given the title of *princeps iuventutis*, "leader of the youth of Rome." No one could have failed to notice that the grandfather and grandsons were now all princeps. The Senate granted Gaius and Lucius the right to hold the consulship in 1 CE and 4 CE, respectively, when they would be twenty-one. We are lucky enough to have a letter written by Augustus to Gaius on September 23, 1 CE. The affection Augustus felt for his grandson is clear, as are his plans:

> Hello my little donkey Gaius,
> heaven knows I miss you whenever
> you are not with me. But my eyes
> long to see my Gaius especially on
> days like today—and wherever you
> are on this day I hope you celebrate

This marble slab bears an inscription known as the Cenotaphia Pisa, a decree in honor of the adopted grandsons of Augutus, Lucius, and Gaius Caesar.

my sixty-fourth birthday by being in good spirits and good health. For as you see, I have got over the sixty-third year, the critical time all old men go through. But I beg the gods that whatever time is left to me, may we be given the grace to spend that time safely with our country flourishing, with you and Lucius grown up and mature and preparing to take on my role.

Augustus's hopes for Gaius and Lucius were not to be fulfilled. In 2 CE, Lucius died, followed by Gaius in 4 CE. Tiberius, who had come back to Rome in 2 CE, was now Augustus's most likely successor. He was once more given the powers of a tribune. And in June 4 CE, Tiberius was officially adopted by Augustus. Agrippa's third son, Posthumus, was briefly considered but did not measure up to Augustus's standards. Augustus was looking much further ahead. Although Tiberius already had a son called Drusus, Augustus made him adopt another son, Germanicus, the eldest child of Tiberius's brother Drusus. After the deaths of Lucius and Gaius within eighteen months of each other, Augustus was taking no chances. He wanted to ensure that there was another generation of the imperial family already in place.

Augustus was widely reported to have disliked Tiberius, and there is evidence for this in his reluctance to make him his heir until there was no other option. Countering this supposition are the letters Augustus wrote to Tiberius, which show nothing but affection. When news came of the disastrous defeat of three Roman legions under Varus in Germany in 9 CE, Rome was facing a real crisis. The effect on the people of Rome was very powerful, and Augustus himself cried out to the inept general who had lost so many men, "Quinctilius Varus, give back my legions!" Tiberius was the one who set out for Germany and brought the situation under control. This was a critical display of his authority to Augustus and to Rome. His right to succeed Augustus was thus confirmed, although, as we shall see, there was a small string attached to Augustus's will.

THE EMPEROR AND HIS LEGACY

It is often difficult to cut through the larger-than-life reputations of powerful leaders and find out who they are as people. This is especially true for leaders of the ancient world who left behind few records themselves. Little has survived of anything Augustus himself wrote. Again, posterity has been fortunate to have more detailed accounts from Suetonius, including Augustus's physical characteristics. He wrote:

> He had bright and shining eyes, and liked to have it thought that there was some sort of divine power in them. He was pleased if someone at whom he looked rather sharply dropped their gaze as if at the brightness of the sun. When he was old, he could not see so well out of

the left eye. His teeth were spaced out and small and not too nice. His hair was wavy and fairish; his ears of an ordinary size. His nose jutted at the top and turned down at the end. His coloring was between dark and fair. He was short, but so well-proportioned that it was not noticeable, unless someone taller were standing next to him… He was not as strong in his left hip, thigh, and leg as his right, and often limped because of this.

In many ways, Augustus took care

The Flaminio Obelisk, built around the thirteenth century BCE, was transported to Rome in 10 BCE by order of Augustus.

to live a very simple life. He liked plain, everyday food like bread, fruit, fish, and cheese. He was also very careful not to drink too much wine. He wore clothes that had been woven in his own household by Octavia, Livia, or Julia, or by one of his grand-daughters. Suetonius says, rather disapprovingly:

> The modesty of his household goods
> and furnishings is clear even now
> from those tables and couches that
> are still around, most of which are
> only just fit for a private citizen.

After decades of restoration, the home of Augustus, boasting these colorful frescoes, was opened to the public for the first time in March 2008.

Even in his speech, Augustus kept to what was plain and simple. Like everyone, he had some favorite expressions, faithfully noted by Suetonius. Some of these have a very homely ring to them, such as the phrase "quicker than boiled asparagus" to express something that happens very speedily, or, to express that he was feeling listless, "I feel like a beet root."

PATRONAGE

The world of a Roman politician was a very open one. Every morning, there was a daily ceremony called the *salutatio* (the greeting). People who were under an obligation of some kind to Augustus would regularly call at his house on the Palatine Hill, in a system based on patronage, which means soliciting the support of a powerful or wealthy person. This system worked at all levels of society. The man under the obligation was called the client, and the man visited by clients was the patron. Augustus, at the top of the heap, was a patron to the whole of Rome, and many people would call to ask for favors. It was an accepted part of Roman society that the patron's house would be open in

PUBLIC (AND PRIVATE) MORALS

On the whole, Augustus seemed able to cope very well with being the focus of attention. He once wrote to Tiberius, who had clearly been upset by some gossip:

> Don't give in to your youthful impulses and complain too much that someone is saying nasty things about me. If no one is doing nasty things to us, that is good enough.

But one disadvantage of this openness was that Augustus's personal life was often in the limelight, and in one area in particular it caused some problems. Augustus had decided early on to do something to reform public morals. In 18 bce, for example, he passed laws that tried to encourage people to get married, stay faithful, and have children. Some Romans may have resented Augustus for trying to do this, for as Suetonius sorrowfully says:

> Not even his friends deny that he committed adultery, though they excuse him by saying that he did it not out of lust but deliberate intent to find out more easily what his opponents were planning, using their women.

However his friends excused him, Augustus does not appear in too good a light here. The Senate enjoyed a neat revenge on him, according to the historian Dio, when he was telling them to keep their wives in order.

He told them, "You ought to advise and to order your wives in the way you like—that's what I do." On hearing this they bothered him all the more, wanting to know what advice he gave Livia.

No doubt the last thing Augustus was prepared to do was share details of how he kept a lady as formidable as Livia in line. When he had tried to reproach Mark Antony over his affair with Cleopatra, Antony replied in very forthright terms:

What's made you change your tune? My affair with the queen? She's my wife. After all, have I only just started it or has it been going on for nine years now? Are you sleeping with just Livia? If, by the time you read this letter, you haven't had Tertulla or Terentilla or Rufilla or Salvia or all of them, then good luck to you. Does where or who matter?

the morning for these clients to call, and Suetonius tells us that Augustus was no different:

> His morning salutatio was open to everyone, even the common people, and he would listen to the requests of those who came with such friendliness that, when one man was hesitating over handing him a request,

Many examples of Roman culture and spectacle, such as the chariot races depicted here, would live on during the reign of Augustus.

Augustus gave him a mock-reproof saying, "It's as if you were giving a penny to an elephant."

DEATH OF AN EMPEROR

The Age of Augustus was viewed by later Romans as Rome's golden age. Augustus led a long, hard-

working life, which in the end was dedicated solely to his city and the structure of political power he established. Everything and everyone else along the way was sacrificed when Rome demanded that sacrifice—Cicero, Antony, Julia; friends, enemies, and family. Augustus was single-minded, and that single-mindedness meant that he must have been a lonely figure, the only man at the top of the pyramid of power he had built. He had outlived most of his friends—Octavia, Agrippa, Maecenas, and Virgil—by many years.

He died at the age of seventy-five in the town of Nola, near Naples. His body was brought from Nola to Rome, with the leading men of each town carrying it in relays. Rome's grief was extravagant. Augustus had a magnificent funeral, and his remains were laid to rest in a huge tomb called a mausoleum, which you can still see today on the banks of the River Tiber. Like his uncle, Julius Caesar, he was deified.

Among his papers Augustus left the *Res Gestae*, instructions for his funeral, a statement of the position of the empire, and his will. He left money to be handed out to the Roman people and to the army, and he made his stepson, Tiberius, the major beneficiary of his will. Poor Tiberius did not get the support he might have expected, however, for in his will Augustus made Tiberius his heir by saying:

> Since cruel fortune has robbed me
> of my sons Gaius and Lucius, I make
> Tiberius Caesar my heir.

There is nothing like knowing you were the second choice. This is one of the reasons why many people since have thought that Augustus disliked

This illustration shows the release of an eagle into the air during the funeral of Augustus, a symbol of the immortal soul of the deceased emperor set free from his body.

Tiberius. And Tiberius went on to earn one of the worst reputations of all the Roman emperors.

Livia was granted the title Augusta to honor her long marriage to Augustus. She lived for fifteen more years and was deified in 41 AD. Augustus and Livia had no children together, but through Tiberius, Drusus, and Julia their grandchildren and descendants ruled Rome for several generations. First came Tiberius, then the grandson of Drusus and Antonia, Emperor Gaius, known to us by his childhood nickname, Caligula. After Gaius came Claudius, the elderly and lame son of Drusus and Antonia, assumed by most of Rome to be rather stupid because he suffered several disabilities. Finally, Augustus's great-great-nephew, the emperor Nero, died without an heir, and the dynasty of Augustus and Livia, called the Julio-Claudians by modern historians, died with him.

The title "Caesar" has lived on into modern times in the titles "Kaiser" and "Czar." That is not Augustus's only legacy to the world. Virgil's poetry is studied the world over. The architecture of Augustan Rome has had a great influence on much of Western culture. The eighth month of the year is still called August in the Western world. The consolidation of power that Augustus brought about was a logical outcome for a civilization that, even as a republic, drew its resources from conquered peoples. Rome's real power came from her legions and the ambitious men who commanded them. Augustus was the first such man to take all political power for himself and hold on to it. But in the process, he created the "glory that was Rome."

A NOTE ABOUT SOURCES

The *Res Gestae* is a very important source for information on Augustus's life because it tells us what he wanted us to know and what he thought was important. A few of Augustus's letters and sayings have also survived.

Augustus was also written about by a great many people in the ancient world. The most important is Suetonius, who wrote about the first twelve leaders to take the name Caesar. In the second century CE, Suetonius worked for the emperor Hadrian as a secretary for a time, so he had access to all sorts of records kept in the Imperial Archives. The period of Augustus's rule was also covered by later historians like Dio and Tacitus.

Monuments to the reign of Augustus exist not only in Rome, but in many of the former provinces of the Roman Empire throughout the Mediterranean World.

We also have some written material from people like Cicero and Velleius Paterculus, who were alive during Augustus's lifetime and even took part in the events of the period. Cicero formed a close friendship with Augustus when Augustus was a young man, while Velleius was a soldier under Augustus and his stepson, Tiberius. Also important as sources are physical objects such as coins and buildings. Coins survive the centuries, and the picture and inscription on a coin can tell us a great deal about the man who had it minted. On the whole, the events of Augustus's reign are well documented, and we have a fair amount of accurate information about him as a person as well as a political leader.

Campus Martius The "Field of Mars," an area north of Rome where its military performed practice drills.

censor An official charged with ensuring public morality, maintaining the census, and overseeing certain financial matters for the government .

consul The top position in Roman government, held simultaneously by two men.

cursus honorum A series of posts that ambitious senators had to hold in order to rise through the political ranks.

dictator A leader with absolute power; in Rome, such a leadership post was only supposed to be temporary, to deal with an immediate crisis.

equites The lower of two aristocratic classes of Roman society, originally drawn from the ranks of Roman cavalrymen.

Forum Romanum The heart of ancient Rome, where important government buildings and monuments were grouped together.

legion A unit of the Roman military, usually about five thousand to six thousand men.

obelisk An upright, four-sided stone pillar that gradually tapers and is topped by a pyramid.

praetor The second office from the top of the *cursus honorum*, praetors usually supervised legal matters.

princeps "Leading citizen," a title by which the emperor was addressed.

proscription The announcement that a man is condemned to death (or exile, if he flees).

province An area of the Roman Empire ruled by a governor in the name of the central Roman government.

quaestor The lowest office on the *cursus honorum*; a quaestor often assisted other more senior officials.

res publica Refers to public affairs and government in the Roman Republic.

salutatio A morning ceremony in which clients would visit their patrons.

American Classical League
860 NW Washington Boulevard, Suite A
Hamilton, OH 45013
(513) 529-7741
Website: https://www.aclclassics.org
The American Classical League was founded in 1919
for the purpose of fostering the study of classical
languages in the United States and Canada.

The American Institute for Roman Culture
1101 West 34th Street, Suite 730-174
Austin, TX 78705
(512) 772-1844
Website: http://romanculture.org
The American Institute for Roman Culture works to
preserve and protect Rome's extraordinary and
unique cultural legacy through education, out-
reach, and action.

Classical Association of New England
Department of Classical Studies
Wellesley College
106 Central Street
Wellesley, MA 02481
Website: http://caneweb.org
The Classical Association of New England is the
professional organization for classicists in New
England. Its mission is to foster the study of the

classical world through the association's many activities and resources, including an annual meeting, scholarships, discretionary grants, CANE's own press, and the *New England Classical Journal* (NECJ).

Department of Greek and Roman Studies
University of Victoria
3800 Finnerty Road
Victoria, BC V8P 5C2
Canada
http://www.uvic.ca/humanities/greekroman
The University of Victoria's Department of Greek and Roman Studies offers a wide-ranging, multidisciplinary program combining the study of language, literature, history, and archaeology centered on the ancient Mediterranean world.

Society for the Promotion of Roman Studies
Dr Fiona Haarer
Roman Society
Senate House, Room 252, South Block
Malet Street
London WC1E 7HU
United Kingdom
Website: http://www.romansociety.org
The Roman Society is the leading British organization dedicated to the study of Rome and

the Roman Empire, including its history, archaeology, literature, and art. It has a broad membership, drawn from over forty countries and from all ages and walks of life.

WEBSITES

Because of the changing nature of internet links, Rosen Publishing has developed an online list of websites related to the subject of this book. This site is updated regularly. Please use this link to access this list:

http://www.rosenlinks.com/LANW/augus

FOR FURTHER READING

Bancroft Hunt, Norman. *Living in Ancient Rome* (Living in the Ancient World). New York, NY: Chelsea House, 2008.

Baum, Margaux, and James Thorne. *Julius Caesar* (Leaders of the Ancient World). New York, NY: Rosen Publishing, 2017.

Cohn, Jessica. *The Ancient Romans* (Crafts from the Past). New York, NY: Gareth Stevens, 2012.

Dando-Collins, Stephen. *Legions of Rome*. London, United Kingdom: Quercus, 2013.

Everitt, Anthony. *Augustus: The Life of Rome's First Emperor*. New York, NY: Random House, 2006.

Goldsworthy, Adrian. *Augustus*. New Haven, CT: Yale University Press, 2015.

Greenblatt, Miriam. *Augustus and Imperial Rome* (Rulers and Their Times). New York, NY: Cavendish Square, 2000.

Kulikowski, Michael. *The Triumph of Empire: The Roman World from Hadrian to Constantine* (History of the Ancient World). Cambridge, MA: Harvard University Press, 2016.

Manolaraki, Eleni. *A History of Rome*. Hoboken, NJ: Wiley-Blackwell, 2009.

Stevenson, Tom. *Julius Caesar and the Transformation of the Roman Republic*. New York, NY: Routledge, 2014

Suetonius. *The Twelve Caesars*. New York, NY: New American Library/Penguin-Putnam, 1993.

Appian. *Roman History: The Civil Wars.* Cambridge, MA: Harvard University Press, 1979.

Augustus. *Res Gestae.* Oxford, United Kingdom: Oxford University Press, 1967.

Cassius Dio. *The Roman History.* Cambridge, MA: Harvard University Press, 1924.

Chisholm, Kitty, and John Ferguson, eds. *Rome, the Augustan Age.* Oxford, United Kingdom: Oxford University Press, 1981.

Cicero. *Philippics.* Oxford, United Kingdom: Clarendon Press, 1900.

Ehrenberg and Jones. *Documents Illustrating the Reigns of Augustus and Tiberius.* Oxford, United Kingdom: Oxford University Press, 1976.

Everitt, Anthony. *Augustus: The Life of Rome's First Emperor.* New York, NY: Random House, 2006.

Jones, A. H. M. *Augustus.* London, United Kingdom: Chatto & Windus, 1977.

Manolaraki, Eleni. *A History of Rome.* Hoboken, NJ: Wiley-Blackwell, 2009.

Paterculus Velleius. *History of Rome.* Cambridge, MA: Harvard University Press, 1979.

Plutarch. *Life of Antony.* London, United Kingdom: William Heinemann, 1920.

Southern, Pat. *Augustus.* London, United Kingdom: Routledge, 1998.

Suetonius. *The Lives of the Caesars.* London, United Kingdom: William Heinemann Ltd, 1924.

Syme, Ronald. *The Roman Revolution*. Oxford, United Kingdom: Oxford University Press, 1960.

Tacitus. *The Annals*. Oxford, United Kingdom: Clarendon Press, 1897.

Virgil. *The Aeneid*. New York, NY: Penguin Classics, 2008.

Webster, Graham. *The Roman Army*. Chester, United Kingdom: Grosvenor Museum Publications, 1973.

ABOUT THE AUTHORS

Margaux Baum is an editor and author of young adult educational books from Queens, New York.

Fiona Forsyth studied classics at Somerville College, Oxford University. She now teaches classics at the Manchester Grammar School in England.

PHOTO CREDITS

Cover, pp. 3, 16–17, 32 DEA/A. Dagli Orti/De Agostini/Getty Images; cover (background), pp. 66–67, 68–69 De Agostini Picture Library/Getty Images p. 7 Gregor Schuster/Photographer's Choice/ Getty Images; pp. 19, 44, 94–95, 100 Print Collector/Hulton Archive/ Getty Images; p. 23 Print Collector/Hulton Fine Art Collection/Getty Images; p. 29 Julian Starks/Moment Open/Getty Images; pp. 34–35 Antonio Vassilacchi/Getty Images; pp. 37, 81, 97 Hulton Archive/ Getty Images; pp. 38–39 Heritage Images/Hulton Fine Art Collection/Getty Images; p. 42 DEA/J. E. Bulloz/De Agostini/Getty Images; p. 47 Phooey/E+/Getty Images; p. 53 Robert Alexander/Archive Photos/Getty Images; p. 58 Kean Collection/Archive Photos/Getty Images; p. 61 Private Collection/© Look and Learn/Elgar Collection/Bridgeman Images; p. 71 Culture Club/Hulton Archive/Getty Images; p. 75 Danita Delimont/Gallo Images/Getty Images; p. 79 Heritage Images/Hulton Archive/Getty Images; p. 85 DEA/S. Vannini/De Agostini/Getty Images; p. 89 Fred Matos/Moment Open/ Getty Images; p. 90 Eric Vandeville/Gamma-Rapho/Getty Images; interior pages background images © iStockphoto.com/kikkalek5050 (sky), Triff/Shutterstock.com (map)

Designer: Brian Garvey; Editor: Philip Wolny; Photo Researcher: Philip Wolny